BLAZERS

Gross History

Gross FACTS About the U.S. CIVIL WAR

BY MIRA VONNE

CAPSTONE PRESS
a capstone imprint

Blazers Books are published by Capstone Press,
1710 Roe Crest Drive, North Mankato, Minnesota 56003
www.mycapstone.com

Library of Congress Cataloging-in-Publication Data
Names: Vonne, Mira, author.
Title: Gross facts about the American Civil War / by Mira Vonne.
Description: North Mankato, Minnesota : Blazers, an imprint of Capstone
    Press, 2017. | Series: Gross history | Includes bibliographical references
    and index. | Audience: Grades 4-6.
Identifiers: LCCN 2016032450| ISBN 9781515741558 (library binding) | ISBN
    9781515741725 (pbk.)
Subjects: LCSH: United States—History—Civil War, 1861-1865—Juvenile
    literature. | United States—History—Civil War, 1861-1865—Social
    aspects—Juvenile literature. | Confederate States of America—Social
    conditions—Juvenile literature. | Soldiers—United States—History—19th
    century—Juvenile literature. | Soldiers—Confederate States of
    America—Juvenile literature.
Classification: LCC E468 .V68 2017 | DDC 973.7—dc23
LC record available at https://lccn.loc.gov/2016032450

Editorial Credits
Mandy Robbins, editor; Philippa Jenkins, designer; Wanda Winch, media researcher;
Steve Walker, production specialist

Photo Credits
Bridgeman Images: Private Collection/Don Troiani, cover, 9, 19, 21; Getty Images: Hulton Archive,
7, Tria Giovan, 12 (right); Granger, NYC – All rights reserved, 5, 11; Library of Congress: Prints and
Photographs Division, 13, 15, 17, 23, 25, 27; North Wind Picture Archives, 29; Philippa Jenkins,
mealworms; Shutterstock: irin-k, fly design, kttpngart, 14, Kuttelvaserova Stuchelova, 28 (rat),
Milan M, color splotch design, monkeystock, grunge drip design, Produck, slime bubbles design,
Protasov AN, weevil, head lice, parasites, Ron Hoenson, 8 (right), schankz, 6, Spectral-Design, 18

Essential content terms are **bold** and are defined on the page where they first appear.

Printed in the United States   5061

TABLE OF CONTENTS

The War Begins

The Civil War (1861-1865) began with a blast. **Confederate** troops fired **cannons** at Fort Sumter on April 12. Northerners quickly joined the Union army. Both sides were ready to fight. They knew conditions could be gross.

Confederate—a person who supported the South during the American Civil War

cannon—a large, heavy piece of artillery, typically mounted on wheels

Uncomfortable Uniforms

Soldiers' uniforms were rarely washed. They stunk from sweat and mud and looked like dirty rags. Jackets and pants were ripped and spotted with blood. Soldiers didn't wash their underwear or socks for months at a time.

Gross Fact

Soldiers rarely got replacement clothing. They took jackets, pants, or boots off the dead.

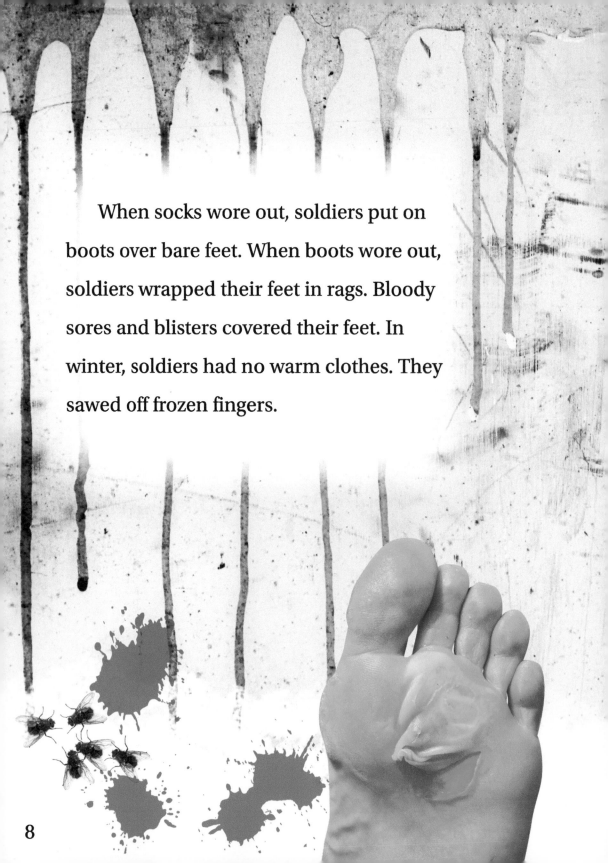

When socks wore out, soldiers put on boots over bare feet. When boots wore out, soldiers wrapped their feet in rags. Bloody sores and blisters covered their feet. In winter, soldiers had no warm clothes. They sawed off frozen fingers.

Long, Cold Nights

Lucky soldiers slept in canvas tents. But most laid on blankets on the ground. If it was wet, the blankets got soggy. Mosquitoes buzzed and bit all night. Lice crawled on the men's blankets, clothing, beards, and hair.

A Disgusting Dinner

Hardtack was common food for soldiers. These crackers were called "teeth dullers" because they were so hard. They often had **maggots** in them. Soldiers dipped the crackers in coffee to soften them and kill the bugs.

maggot—the larva of certain flies

hardtack

Meat was scarce for soldiers. Depending on what was available, soldiers ate cow, horse, mule, and even rat meat. Salt helped **preserve** meat. But often the meat was rotten.

preserve—to protect something so that it stays in its original condition

rotten meat

15

Deadly Weapons

Civil War soldiers shot rifles. Their lead bullets exploded when they hit bone. The closer the bullet's **impact**, the more damage it caused.

impact—the action of one object coming forcibly into contact with another

Cross Fact

The Battle of Antietam was the bloodiest day of the American Civil War. Nearly 23,000 men were killed, wounded, or captured.

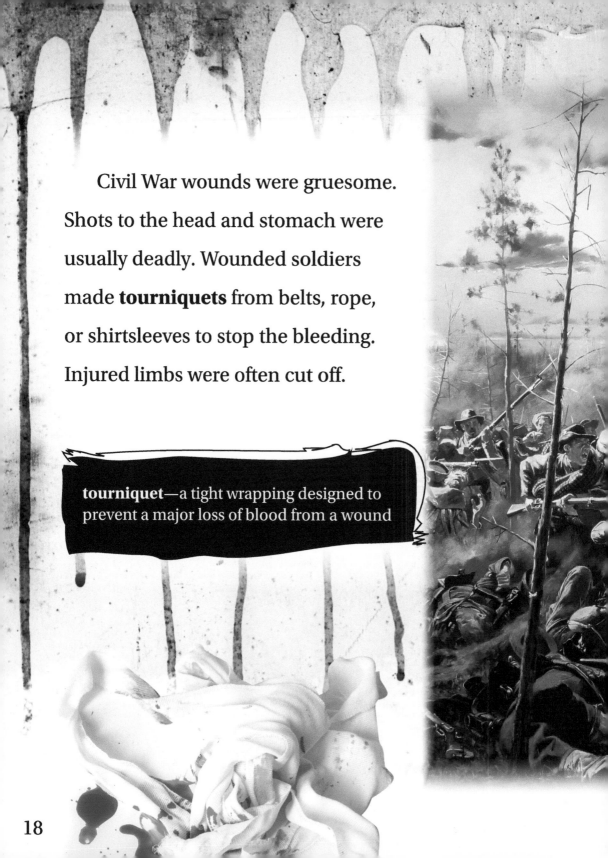

Civil War wounds were gruesome. Shots to the head and stomach were usually deadly. Wounded soldiers made **tourniquets** from belts, rope, or shirtsleeves to stop the bleeding. Injured limbs were often cut off.

tourniquet—a tight wrapping designed to prevent a major loss of blood from a wound

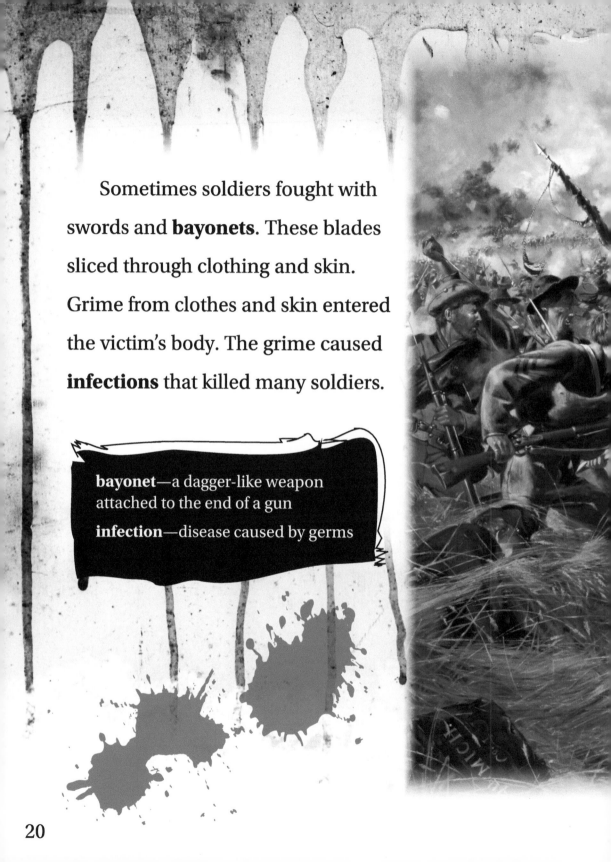

Sometimes soldiers fought with swords and **bayonets**. These blades sliced through clothing and skin. Grime from clothes and skin entered the victim's body. The grime caused **infections** that killed many soldiers.

bayonet—a dagger-like weapon attached to the end of a gun

infection—disease caused by germs

Battling Germs

If soldiers washed at all, they did it in the same water they drank. Drinking dirty water caused **dysentery** and other diseases. Disease spread easily during war. Sickness made living conditions worse.

dysentery—a sometimes deadly infection of the intestines that can cause diarrhea

Gross Fact

More soldiers died from diarrhea than were killed in battle during the American Civil War.

Soldiers dug trenches to use as toilets. These stinky dirt pits were often dug close to the camp's water and food supply. Human waste piled up. If the waste wasn't covered with dirt, flies became a big problem.

Field Hospitals

Hospitals were set up near the battlefields. They were very crowded. Doctors had few supplies and little clean water. **Amputation** was the most common treatment for soldiers. They were done with little or no **anesthesia**.

amputation—cutting off someone's arm, leg, or other body part, usually because the part is damaged

anesthesia—a gas or injection that prevents pain during treatments and operations

Cross Fact

More than 70 percent of the patients treated had injuries to their arms or legs.

Prison Horrors

Captured soldiers went to prison camps with filthy conditions. Flies, maggots, and lice lived on the men. Prisoners received little food. These men were probably the most relieved when the awful war was over.

Glossary

amputation (am-pyuh-TAY-shun)—cutting off someone's arm, leg, or other body part, usually because the part is damaged

anesthesia (a-nuhs-THEE-zhuh)—a gas or injection that prevents pain during treatments and operations

bayonet (BAY-uh-net)—a dagger-like weapon attached to the end of a gun

cannon (KAN-uhn)—a large, heavy piece of artillery, typically mounted on wheels

Confederate (kuhn-FE-der-uht)—a person who supported the South during the Civil War

dysentery (DI-sen-tayr-ee)—a sometimes deadly infection of the intestines that can cause diarrhea

impact (IM-pakt)—the action of one object coming forcibly into contact with another

infection (in-FEK-shuhn)—disease caused by germs

maggot (MAG-uht)—the larva of certain flies

preserve (pri-ZURV)—to protect something so that it stays in its original condition

tourniquet (TUR-nuh-ket)—a tight wrapping

Union (YOON-yuhn)—the northern states that fought against the Southern states in the Civil War

Read More

Machajewski, Sarah. *A Kid's Life During the American Civil War*. How Kids Lived. New York: PowerKids Press, 2015.

O'Connor, Jim. *What was the Battle of Gettysburg?* New York: Grosset & Dunlap, 2013.

Ratliff, Thomas. *You Wouldn't Want to be a Civil War Soldier! A War You'd Rather Not Fight.* New York: Franklin Watts, 2013.

Internet Sites

FactHound offers a safe, fun way to find Internet sites related to this book. All of the sites on FactHound have been researched by our staff.

Here's all you do:

Visit *www.facthound.com*

Type in this code: 9781515741558

 **Super-cool stuff!** Check out projects, games and lots more at **www.capstonekids.com**

Critical Thinking Using the Common Core

- The details in this book are gross. What other words can you use to describe life during the Civil War? (Key Ideas and Details)

- How do the images add information about the Civil War? Describe some of these images. (Craft and Structure)

- Compare life during the Civil War with living today. Would you want to live during the Civil War? Why or why not? (Integration of Knowledge and Ideas)

Index